Junior Library of Money

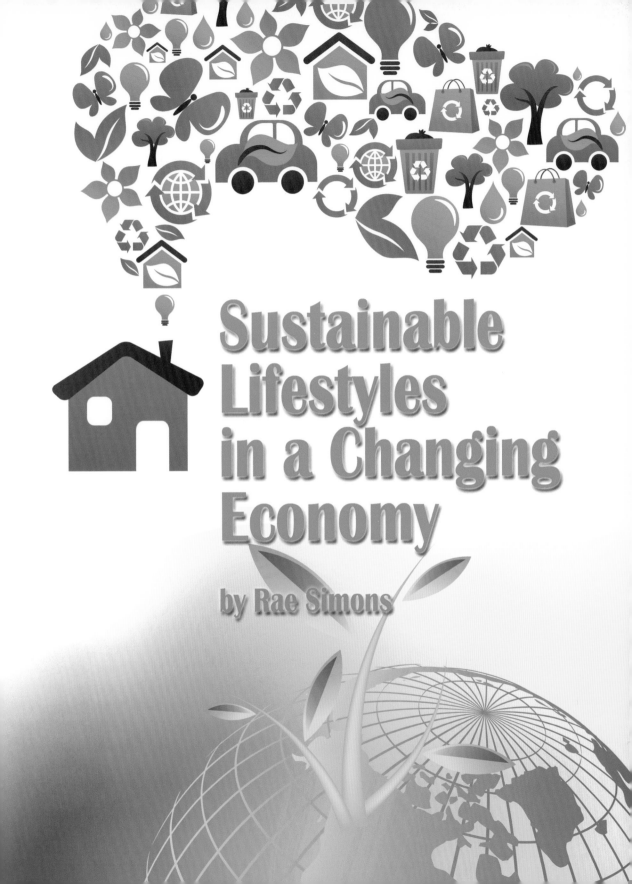

Sustainable Lifestyles in a Changing Economy

by Rae Simons

MASON CREST PUBLISHERS INC.
370 Reed Road
Broomall, Pennsylvania 19008
(866)MCP-BOOK (toll free)
www.masoncrest.com

First Printing
9 8 7 6 5 4 3 2 1

Library of Congress Cataloging-in-Publication Data

Simons, Rae, 1957–
    Sustainable lifestyles in a changing economy / by Rae Simons.
        p. cm.
    Includes bibliographical references and index.
    ISBN 978-1-4222-1771-9 (hbk.)   ISBN 978-1-4222-1759-7 (series)
    ISBN 978-1-4222-1890-7(pbk.)   ISBN 978-1-4222-1878-5 (pbk. series)
    1. Sustainable living—Economic aspects. 2. Environmentalism—Economic aspects.
    I. Title.
    GE196.S56 2011
    640—dc22
                                2010027817

Design by Wendy Arakawa.
Produced by Harding House Publishing Service, Inc.
www.hardinghousepages.com
Cover design by Torque Advertising and Design.
Printed by Bang Printing.

CONTENTS

INTRODUCTION

Our lives interact with the global financial system on an almost daily basis: we take money out of an ATM machine, we use a credit card to go shopping at the mall, we write a check to pay the rent, we apply for a loan to buy a new car, we set something aside in a savings account, we hear on the evening news whether the stock market went up or down. These interactions are not just frequent, they are consequential. Deciding whether to attend college, buying a house, or saving enough for retirement, are decisions with large financial implications for almost every household. Even small decisions like using a debit or a credit card become large when made repeatedly over time.

And yet, many people do not understand how to make good financial decisions. They do not understand how inflation works or why it matters. They do not understand the long-run costs of using consumer credit. They do not understand how to assess whether attending college makes sense, or whether or how much money they should borrow to do so. They do not understand the many different ways there are to save and invest their money and which investments make the most sense for them.

And because they do not understand, they make mistakes. They run up balances they cannot afford to repay on their credit card. They drop out of high school and end up unemployed or trying to make ends meet on a minimum wage job, or they borrow so much to pay for college that they are drowning in debt when they graduate. They don't save enough. They pay high interests rates and fees when lower cost options are available. They don't buy insurance to protect themselves from financial risks. They find themselves declaring bankruptcy, with their homes in foreclosure.

We can do better. We must do better. In an increasingly sophisticated financial world, everyone needs a basic knowledge of our financial system. The books in this series provide just such a foundation. The series has individual books devoted specifically to the financial decisions most relevant to children: work, school, and spending money. Other books in the series introduce students to the key institutions of our financial system:

money, banks, the stock market, the Federal Reserve, the FDIC. Collectively they teach basic financial concepts: inflation, interest rates, compounding, risk vs. reward, credit ratings, stock ownership, capitalism. They explain how basic financial transactions work: how to write a check, how to balance a checking account, what it means to borrow money. And they provide a brief history of our financial system, tracing how we got where we are today.

There are benefits to all of us of having today's children more financially literate. First, if we can help the students of today start making wise financial choices when they are young, they can hopefully avoid the financial mishaps that have been so much in the news of late. Second, as the financial crisis of 2007–2010 has shown, poor individual financial choices can sometimes have implications for the health of the overall financial system, something that affects everyone. Finally, the financial system is an important part of our overall economy. The students of today are the business and political leaders of tomorrow. We need financially literate citizens to choose the leaders who will guide our economy through the inevitable changes that lie ahead.

Brigitte Madrian, Ph.D.
Aetna Professor of Public Policy
and Corporate Management
Harvard Kennedy School

What Is a Sustainable Lifestyle?

Everywhere you go, you hear about being "green." You can buy green bags, green shirts, green cars, and green cleaning supplies. But what does that even mean, exactly? You probably already know that it has something to do with helping the environment, but all those advertisements for green products can leave you pretty confused.

Green products all have to do with the idea of sustainability. Sustainability, as defined by the United Nations, is a behavior or item that "meets the needs of the present without compromising the needs of the future." In other words, sustainability means that everyone living today should have comfortable, happy lives, but shouldn't use so many resources to be comfortable and happy that we doom future generations to unhappiness.

As you might guess, achieving that goal is pretty tricky. Many of us are not even close to living sustainable lives. We buy lots of stuff we don't need, we use energy wastefully, and we often pollute the environment, even if we don't mean to. Fortunately, there are lots of steps we can take to start living more sustainably. Sustainable living is a lifestyle that reduces your use of the Earth's natural resources, and also reduces the use of your own personal resources.

There are lots of different dimensions to sustainability. We can talk about sustainable energy, sustainable agriculture, and even sustainable finances. It turns out that saving money has a lot to do with saving the Earth! A lot of what we spend our money on today is unsustainable: gas-guzzling cars, huge houses, new clothes every month, and food that we just end up throwing out because it goes bad before we can eat it.

The goal of this book is to introduce you to ways that you can start saving money and practicing sustainable finances. At the same time, these very same practices help the environment by using fewer resources and creating less waste. Now that's a win-win situation.

What Do You Really Need to Live?

The first step to living a more sustainable life is to figure out what you really need to live. Needs are things that a person has to have in order to survive and have a basically happy life. There are both physical and psychological components to needs. They are pretty universal—people everywhere have the same needs, no matter where they live, what sort of government they have, or what they look like.

Humans need the following things to lead happy, healthy lives:

- food and water
- clothing
- shelter, including a roof over your head, utilities, and furniture
- transportation
- health care
- education
- relationships with other people, including family and friends
- a sense of safety and security

If people don't have these things, they're probably in trouble. People can't survive for long periods of time without physical, basic necessities like food, water, or shelter. Without psychological necessities like security or relationships, people become unhappy and mentally unbalanced.

Being sustainable does not mean that you give up any of these basic necessities. The definition of sustainability, along with common sense and human rights, declares that all human beings should have access to necessities, so that they can live healthy, happy, and fulfilled lives.

What Don't You Really Need to Live?

While there are lots of things that we need to survive as humans, there are also a lot of things we definitely don't need. These are called wants. Wants are things that are nice to have, but aren't really required to help us survive, or even to make us truly satisfied with our lives. Some wants include:

- TV
- video games
- new clothes all the time
- eating out in restaurants
- vacations
- drugs or alcohol
- pets
- makeup
- gifts
- mp3 players

Some of these things probably make you happy and might seem like absolute necessities. You always look forward to that family summer vacation to the beach, you couldn't live without watching your favorite TV show, and you love your cat and dog like family. But if you take a good look at that list of wants, you'll realize that none of them help you survive. As long as you have food, shelter, and a loving family or set of friends, then you've got all the basics covered. Wants are just icing on the cake, things that make life a little more fun.

Don't worry, you don't have to give up everything on your list of wants in order to live a sustainable life. You should, however, be able to identify which things in your life are wants, and which are needs. You might have to learn to live without some of your wants, or to find alternatives for some of them, which are more friendly to both the environment and your wallet.

The point of sustainability is not to give up everything you love. Sustainability is about figuring out how to be happy because you have everything you need, plus really appreciating having some of the things you want, if you have the money for them and if having them doesn't make anyone else worse off. In the long run, you'll be saving yourself a lot of money, and you'll be making the world a better place for yourself, for the other billions of human beings on the planet, and for the Earth.

The Effects of Unsustainable Living on Your Finances

Unsustainable money management, simply put, means that you're spending more money than you have, or hope to have in the very near future. It's sustainability at a personal level, since you are only concerned with sustainability as it applies to one individual: you. You have to live within your means today, so that you can be happy in the future.

There are lots of reasons to practice sustainable finances. Let's say you really want a new video game that just came out. It's $60, but you only have $20 to spend right now. What do you do? If you follow the unsustainable path, you might ask your sister if you can borrow the extra $40. After you buy it, you realize you can't pay her back because you don't have any more money, and your birthday isn't for another three months. You're definitely in trouble. On the other hand, if you decide to handle your purchase sustainably, you have a couple options. You can wait the three months until you get some birthday money, or you can search around for a used game for $20. You could even just play it at one of your friend's houses until you can afford it; then maybe you'll realize you don't even like it that much and don't need to buy it.

Unsustainable money management can have a lot more serious consequences then just making your sister angry at you. If you're spending too much money on a credit card, for example, not paying off your purchases is bad news. Credit cards work by letting you pay for things before you actually have the money for them. You then have to pay off your debts within a limited amount of time, usually a month or so. If you don't have the money, you'll get calls from the credit card company, and eventually a debt collector. You'll have to pay even more money in late fees, and you'll have a lot of trouble getting another credit card or a loan later on. Your **credit report**, a statement of your financial activity, will suffer, letting banks and companies know that you aren't responsible with your money.

THE EFFECTS OF UNSUSTAINABLE LIVING ON THE PLANET

Unsustainable living doesn't just have a negative effect on your money; it also affects the planet. Practicing sustainable living in all areas of your life makes a difference, especially if you do it along with a lot of other people. All together, using up more resources than we need is leading to lots of environmental and social problems.

Climate change is closely tied to sustainability. Basically, all of our cars, machines, houses, and industries pump a lot of carbon dioxide into the air, which traps heat in the Earth's atmosphere. Climate change will have terrible consequences for the enviroment, including people, in the future, as droughts increase, sea levels rise, and animals and plants die out. Scientists know that climate change is happening— it isn't really a debate anymore. Sure, it's impossible to predict exactly how much or in what ways the planet is going to change, but most experts agree that human actions are causing the Earth to warm up.

Other unsustainable actions include polluting rivers and lakes, using chemical fertilizers to grow lawns and crops, cutting down forests, and overhunting animals. All of these things have the distinct potential to cause harm, not only to the environment, but to people too.

For example, factories often pump waste into rivers because it's cheaper than getting rid of it sustainably. However, in the long run, these actions can be very harmful. The pollution could make people sick, kill fish and other river life, and ruin thousands of fishermen's lives, not to mention that the company could get sued or shut down for violating pollution laws. It turns out that a little extra effort in sustainably getting rid of the waste would have been a lot easier than dealing with the consequences of polluting. The point is that sustainable living isn't always easy or obvious, but it's definitely worth it.

Roadblocks to a Sustainable Lifestyle

Living sustainably definitely isn't easy, if you've never tried it before. There are lots of obstacles in the way of living a truly sustainable life, but that doesn't mean you shouldn't try hard to get past them.

One of the biggest roadblocks to sustainable living is simply your habits. If you're used to keeping the lights on in every room in your house all the time, or if you always throw your plastic bottles in the garbage instead of the recycling, it'll be hard to break those habits. Even if you really want to start living more sustainably, you'll have to continually remind yourself of your bad habits. Keep notes for yourself around your house or have other people remind you to do small

tasks. Stick some Post-it notes by every light switch in your house, and get your environmentally conscious friend to remind you to recycle at school.

It's hard to live sustainably if no one else around you is. Your social life will probably get in the way of living sustainably from time to time, when your friends invite you to go out to eat once or twice every week, or to go shopping. You'll have to figure out how you can still have fun with your friends but stay away from spending too much money at the ice cream shop or the mall. That could mean more window shopping, smaller coffees, and experiments with home cooking. Make your quest to live sustainably fun! Include your friends and do things you enjoy, and you'll be much more likely to stick to your goals.

A third obstacle you might encounter is deciding which things in your life are wants and which are needs. It's not always easy to tell, especially because you probably want some things a lot. If your goal is to cut down on spending money and to use up fewer of the Earth's resources, then commit yourself to eliminating a few of your wants. Start small, though, or you might end up thinking your goal of living sustainably is impossible. If your jeans still fit and aren't worn out, for example, don't get another pair just because you happen to be at the mall. (On the other hand, it's still okay to buy clothes once in a while.) Or if your notebooks from school last year are almost empty, reuse them this year rather than buying new ones. At the least, you'll be happy you saved the extra money.

HIGH EXPECTATIONS

You step up to a fast food counter. You know exactly what you want: a double cheeseburger, large fries, and an extra-large soda. It takes only about two minutes to order and receive your food. Plus, it only cost $4.

People today have high expectations that aren't always **realistic** or healthy. We want lots of stuff in a short period of time, preferably for a low price, though that's **negotiable**. We're also always looking for the newest fashion, and the latest thing. You can see this in the popularity of fast-food chains, shopping trips to giant malls, and our fascination with the latest technological gadgets.

Our desire for all this stuff is called consumerism. For a long, long time, people have wanted to acquire new things to make their lives easier. In the past, consumerism was mostly about getting the necessities. Very few people were able to afford luxuries, so what money they did have was spent on medicines, basic clothing, and housing, and maybe an occasional book or hair comb.

Today, most people have at least some **disposable income**, meaning that they have enough money to buy things that aren't necessities. Over the past century or so, people have started buying lots of things they want, both because a lot of products do make our lives easier and more fun, and because consumerism is part of our **culture**.

There are lots of things that tell us to consume. Advertisements on TV, billboards, magazines, movies, and radio constantly tell us to buy more stuff. Holidays like Christmas and Valentine's Day encourage us to get presents for our loved ones. When we're kids, we see everyone around us taking trips to the mall and the grocery store, so we naturally grow up to think that's the way things have to be.

Today, excessive consumerism is a part of our everyday lives, but people are starting to take a good look at consumerism and are finding some problems with it. Manufacturing all the goods that everyone wants uses a lot of resources, including oil, coal, metal, and rock. **Extracting** resources can take a heavy toll on the environment, and limits how much of those resources we can use in the future. Companies also often want to make their goods as cheaply as possible, so they cut corners by treating their workers poorly or damaging the environment.

Finally, it costs a lot of money to always buy new stuff. Not everyone has a lot of money, especially since many countries in the world are now in a **recession**. Since consumerism is so ingrained in people's minds, however, we think we need a new cell phone, new clothes, and a new car, even if we can't really afford them.

Consumerism doesn't have to be such a powerful force. Limiting your purchases to things you need and really want is a good way to start beating consumerism in your own life.

Buying Things You Don't Really Need

Think about how much money you spend on things you don't need. Maybe it's only a little bit, or none at all. Or maybe, like a lot of people, you spend your extra money on a new pair of shoes every few weeks or daily trips to the coffee bar. If you ever find yourself running out of money for the things you need, even though you get a regular allowance or have a part-time job, then you're probably buying too much stuff.

Cutting down on purchases is harder than it sounds. How do you figure out what things to stop buying? Start by keeping a list of everything you buy during one month and how much each thing is. Seeing all your purchases down on paper might inspire you to limit your spending.

Don't make budget cuts that you'll resent. If you see your cuts as sacrifices, you probably won't be successful. You have to replace unsustainable activities with sustainable ones that you enjoy, not ones that will make you grumble about giving up your favorite things.

Do **THINGS** Make You **HAPPY?**

The simple answer is, yes and no. Sometimes buying things makes people happy, but a lot of times, it doesn't. That might come as a surprise, but it's backed up by science.

Recently, psychologists have conducted several studies of consumerism and happiness.

Most found that consumerism and having money make people happy only up to a certain point.

Buying necessities made people happy, since without a house, food, or some clothes, it's hard to live a good life. However, the studies also found that shopping for wants really didn't make people all that happy. Other things, like family, nature, and being liked by others made people far happier than shopping.

The next time you take a trip to the mall, make a note of how you feel before and after. You might be excited to look for some new clothes, and to see your friends, but pay close attention to your emotions and your energy while you're shopping and after you get home. Don't be surprised if you're tired, grumpy, and not feeling satisfied with your trip.

If you realize that buying things doesn't actually make you happier, or even makes you a little less happy, it'll be easier to live sustainably and practice sustainable money management. The next time you're tempted to buy something you don't need or really even want, just remind yourself that you won't be any happier that you purchased it, and you'll have less money for the things that you really do need to buy.

Sustainable Lifestyles in a Changing Economy **25**

Advertisements are everywhere. Ads telling us to buy everything from cars to toys to carrot choppers bombard us from the TV and from the printed page. Over $15 billion is spent on advertisements just for children in the United States. All that money spent on ads pays off, too: U.S. teens spend about $160 billion a year, and children spend $18 billion.

Advertising convinces millions of people to buy things they otherwise wouldn't buy. The people who create ads know how to make their product attractive, and how to make people want to buy it. If you want to spend less, be on the lookout for ads that try to convince you to spend more.

You should be in charge of your money and your choices, so don't let ads try to make choices for you. There's no reason you have to listen to those ads.

BUY!

ADVERTISING

SPEND!

Sustainable Lifestyles in a Changing Economy 27

Goals for Sustainable Living

The end goal of sustainable living is to be happy with what you have right now, and to have enough resources to be happy in the forseeable future. That means a couple of different things.

As far as your finances go, you want to have enough money to buy a few new things without running out of money. At this point, your parents probably buy you most of the things you need, but you might spend some money on a few extra things. Start practicing sustainable finances now, though, so that you're ready for when you're in charge of more of your own money.

The other goal of sustainable living is to reduce your footprint on Earth and to use only your share of the planet's resources, no more. Everything you do has some sort of impact on the environment, so even small steps toward sustainable living are worth it.

If you're interested in figuring out how sustainably you live (and how far you have to go to live even more sustainably), visit sustainability.publicradio.org/consumerconsequences/ for more information. This quiz measures your **footprint** in terms of how much energy you use, what you eat, and where you live. It calculates how many Earths we would need if everyone on the planet lived the way you do. Most people require four or more Earths. It might open your eyes to how much your life really impacts the planet.

Sustainable Lifestyles in a Changing Economy   29

SMALL STEPS: recycle reuse reduce

Recycling is one simple thing you can do to start living sustainably. Recycling reduces the amount of new resources that go into making new things. Everything that's made goes through a process. Take a notebook, for example. In order to make the notebook, a lumber company has to use machines to cut down a tree. The tree is shipped to a factory where it's made into sheets of paper, and bound into a notebook. The notebook is shipped to a store and sold to you. Eventually, you throw the notebook in the trash and buy another one, starting the process all over again. Every time a new notebook is made, another tree is cut down and more energy is used.

Once recycling enters the picture, though, the process of production becomes a closed cycle. If you recycle the notebook, it will be taken to a recycling facility that will sell the paper to the notebook company. The company makes a new notebook out of it and sends it to a store. Then, you buy the recycled notebook, knowing that you prevented a tree from being cut down.

Sometimes, recycling can even save you money. Many states have bottle-return programs, which get you five or ten cents back for every bottle you recycle into special machines that accept bottles and cans. Bottle drives are great ideas for club or team fundraisers. Recycling bottles and cans is also a good addition to your sustainable lifestyle, since you save resources like alumuninum and plastic (which usually comes from oil byproducts), and you earn yourself a little bit of money as a reward.

The rules of recycling can be pretty confusing. Different kinds of plastics have different numbers on them, contained inside those little triangles everyone associates with recycling. Sometimes you can only recycle number 1 and 2 plastics, sometimes only number 5 and 6, and sometimes all types. Things made out of paper and cardboard are also all different. Every community has a different set of guidelines for what you can and can't recycle, which are often hard to remember. Even if you can recycle pizza boxes in your hometown, when you visit your grandma, you might not be able to put those in the recycling bin.

The reason for all this confusion is that each recycling facility pro-cesses different kinds of paper and plastic. It can be expensive to run a facility, and even more expen-sive to run one that can handle every sort of material there is. So in one county, number 2 plastic bottles are fine, but another county isn't equipped to recycle them.

While all this can be really frus-trating, most communities provide lots of information about recycling dos and don'ts. Look up your town's waste manage-ment phone number or website, or see if you can find recycling information on your town's webpage.

SMALL STEPS:
Eat Less Meat

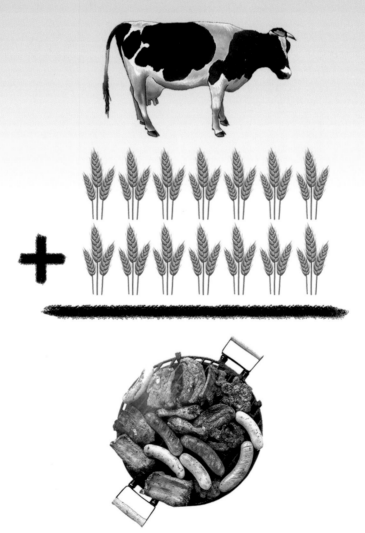

More and more people are eating more and more meat. It used to be that meat was a luxury that families bought once or twice a week. Now, almost every meal has meat in it in some form or another. Meat can be part of a good diet, but too much meat is bad for your health, bad for the environment, and bad for your wallet.

Meat takes a lot more energy to produce than fruits and vegetables. Most of the meat available in supermarkets and restaurants comes from animals that were raised in gigantic feed lots, where they were fed mostly corn and soybeans. Growing animal feed requires a lot of energy and water, not to mention all the oil it takes to harvest it and ship it to where the animals are.

After the animals are slaughtered, it takes even more energy to process them into meat and ship them all over the country to grocery stores and restuarants. All in all, one hamburger takes the same amount of energy as driving a small car twenty miles.

Fortunately, you have a lot of options if you want to avoid eating so much meat. If you really want to lay off the meat, you can become vegetarian or vegan. Vegetarians don't eat meat, while vegans don't eat any animal products, including eggs and dairy. Vegan diets consume one and a half fewer tons of carbon than the average American diet, so cutting the meat out of your diet can have a big impact.

If saying goodbye to meat would just be too hard or isn't something you're interested in, look into buying meat from local farms. The animals at small, rural farms around the country are usually treated well and have been raised sustainably. The meat from local farms doesn't have to be shipped from across the country either. And best of all, fresh, local meat tastes even better than what you're used to eating.

SMALL STEPS: Grow Your Own Vegetables

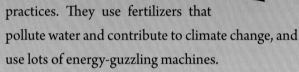

To make your food choices even more sustainable, consider starting a garden. Raising vegetables and fruit and then shipping them across the world uses a lot of energy. Farms that grow hundreds of acres of veggies at a time also don't usually use sustainable agricultural practices. They use fertilizers that pollute water and contribute to climate change, and use lots of energy-guzzling machines.

Buying **organic** produce is one way to make your food purchases more sustainable, but it can get expensive. For a cheaper way to get environmentally friendly vegetables, try growing your own or buying them from a local farmer. It's estimated that about four-fifths of the energy that's used to get a vegetable to your plate comes from shipping it. If all you have to do is pick a tomato from your backyard, it instead took exactly zero gallons of gas to get it to you.

Growing a garden is also great for sustainable living because it's much cheaper than driving to the grocery store to buy your produce. After your initial investment in seeds and garden equipment, your vegetables are free!

SMALL STEPS:

Can, Freeze, and Preserve

Growing a garden and buying local produce is all well and good during the summer, but what about the winter? There's nothing growing, so you might think you'll have to go back to the grocery store and get your produce from who knows where. However, if you're willing to put in a little time and effort, you can eat sustainably all year long.

Canning and preserving is a skill most people associate with their grandmas, but give it a chance. Wouldn't it be nice to eat some homemade tomato sauce made with tomatoes from your garden—in January? Preserving food includes techniques like freezing, pickling, and canning. You can make all kinds of stuff, from pickles to sauces to jams. You have to start preserving produce as you pick it from your garden, but you get to enjoy it during the fall, winter, and spring.

And best of all, you're saving money. Instead of buying jam, peas, frozen fruit for smoothies, and pickles at the supermarket, you're pulling them out for free from your kitchen's pantry or your cellar.

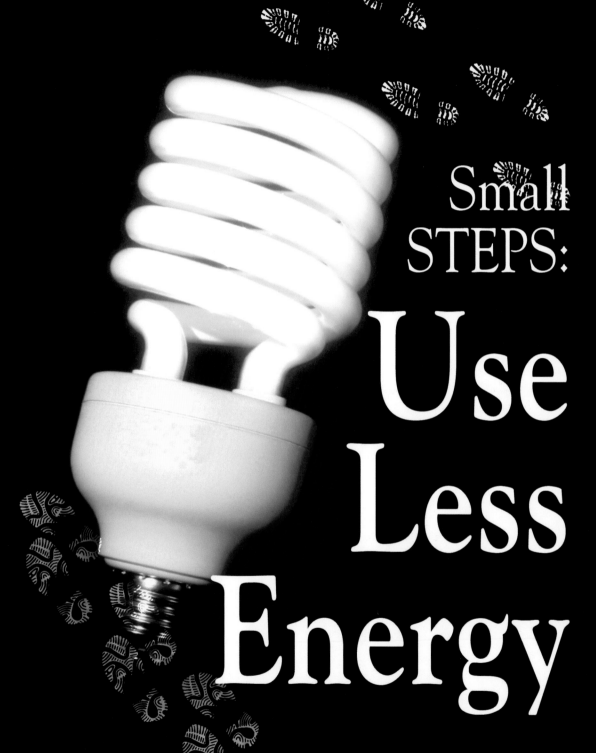

Small STEPS:

Use Less Energy

Turn the lights off when you leave the room! You've probably heard that a million times from your mom or dad. They're on to something—turning off the lights when you're not using them is a good start in sustainable living.

We usually use oil, natural gas, or coal for almost everything we do. Electricity comes from coal, our cars are powered by gasoline, and our heat comes from natural gas. Using all this energy contributes to climate change and eats into our savings, so limiting how much energy we use is a very important part of sustainability. The average American family spends $1,900 a year on utilties like electricity and hot water, so there's definitely room for improvement.

There are lots of ways to reduce energy use. They include:

- Buying energy efficient appliances like washing machines (look for Energy Star labels)
- Using CFL bulbs, which are more energy efficient
- Checking with your energy supplier to see if you can get some of your energy from wind, solar, or hydro power
- Buying a solar panel or small wind turbine to create your own energy for your house
- Unplugging appliances and electronic devices you aren't using; they use up energy when they're just plugged in
- Turning your computer off or setting it to hibernate when you aren't using it
- Setting the thermostat a couple of degrees lower (winter) or higher (summer)
- Using fans instead of air conditioning

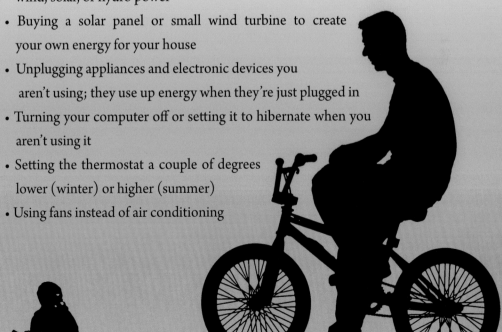

SMALL STEPS:
Shop at Secondhand Stores

Living sustainably doesn't have to mean that you stop buying things for fun. Buying stuff that's new to you lets you enjoy getting new things, but without the worry that you're contributing to environmental damage or wasting your money on expensive things.

Secondhand stores of all kinds exist in most cities and towns. Salvation Army and Goodwill are two secondhand shops that have hundreds of locations around the United States and Canada. Smaller stores that specialize in clothes, books, or antiques can also be found in lots of places. You might want to check out Army Navy surplus stores as well. Garage sales are another place to buy used items, and are fun to hunt around for.

Shopping at secondhand stores gives new life to old things. It's like recycling for clothes and books, instead of bottles and cans. Secondhand things also tend to be a lot cheaper than buying the same thing brand new.

USED BOOKS

Small Steps:
Use
Less
Plastic

A lot of plastic is made from oil **byproducts**, and most things made out of plastic go straight to the dump rather than a recycling facility. There are lots of alternatives to plastic bottles, bags, and packaging, so try some of these suggestions:

- Buy a metal or other resusable water bottle instead of disposable plastic ones
- Take a reusable lunch box and containers to school every day instead of plastic bags
- Bring your own grocery bags to the store, so that you don't have to use plastic bags
- Find alternatives to plastic toothbrushes, pens, and hair combs. Most of these kinds of items come in recyclable forms if you look around.
- Refuse plastic bags at stores when you only buy one small item that you can carry to your car.

If you follow these suggestions, and come up with your own, you'll also save money because you won't be buying water bottles, plastic bags, and other plastic goods over and over again every time you throw them out.

SMALL STEPS: THINK BEFORE YOU BUY

The best way to save yourself money and use up fewer of the Earth's resources is to simply think about everything before you buy it. A lot of our purchases are impulse buys. That means that we see something we like, put it in our shopping cart without thinking it through, and immediately buy it. Stores know how to take advantage of people's willingness to buy things on impulse. Take a look at the rows of candy and small items in supermarket checkout lines. You don't have much time to think about whether you really want that candy bar if you're seconds away from paying for your groceries, so if it catches your eye, it goes straight onto the conveyor belt.

Every time you buy something, think about it. To remind yourself, stick a note in your wallet, if you carry one, or tell your parents or friends to remind you. If you see something you think you might want to buy, and you're going to be in the same store for awhile, don't carry it around with you. If you really want it by the time you're ready to leave, then buy it, but if you decide it's not really worth it, then don't. Better yet, you might have even forgotten about it, which means you didn't really want it in the first place.

Big purchases are even more important to think about. You want to be especially sure that you really like expensive items before you buy them, so that you don't feel like you wasted a lot of money afterward. When buying expensive clothes, new video games, or jewelry, take extra care when thinking about your purchase. There's nothing worse then bringing a $300 mp3 player home and wishing you had chosen the alternative model instead.

Finally, take advantage of return policies. Everyone makes mistakes from time to time, so when you buy something you actually don't really want, find out if you can return it. Most bigger stores let you return things within a limited time. Meanwhile, keep tags on items or keep your purchases unwrapped for a little while if you're still on the fence as to whether you want them or not.

BIG STEPS: CHANGE THE WORLD!

Little steps are important, but if you want to make a bigger change, then take some bigger steps.

The most important thing we can do to live more sustainably is to change **infrastructures** like government, businesses, transportation systems, and schools. Changing the minds of the people in charge, like politicians, the heads of energy companies, and presidents of universities will lead to larger, more effective changes. Once the people who run the world's countries and businesses understand the need for everyone to live sustainably, then they can make big changes in government and in the business world. Think about it: you can buy a fuel efficient car that gets 35 mpg, but you have to make an effort to find one. If there was a law that said all cars must be made so that they get 45 mpg, then you don't have to worry about it, and people will use less gasoline without even thinking.

Individuals can be the driving force behind changing big minds. Write to politicians in the local and federal governments to let them know that you support sustainable policy and laws. The more people who write, the better, so get as many people as you know to write too.

Spread your knowledge about sustainability to other people. Join your school's environmental club, or start one if it doesn't exist. Tell as many people as possible about what you've learned. One of them might one day become a member of Congress or the next owner of a solar power company (or you might yourself!).

BIG STEPS:
GOOD-BYE TO FOSSIL FUELS

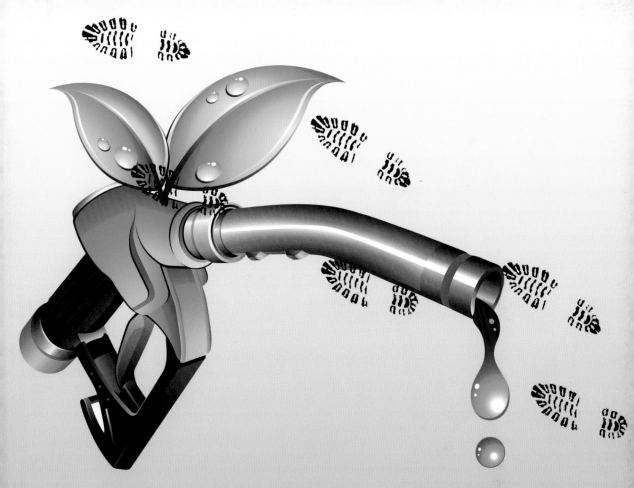

We use a lot of nonrenewable energy sources like oil, coal, and natural gas. Nonrenewable means that when we use them up, they're gone. Right now, we're using up all the oil that can be easily drilled. Eventually, the oil will get harder and harder to find and more expensive to drill, and using oil won't be a choice any more.

Before that happens, we have to use less energy, and switch to renewable energies like wind, hydropower, solar, and biomass. There is essentially a limitless amount of renewable energy, since the sun isn't going to stop shining and the wind isn't going to stop blowing anytime soon. Renewable energy also releases less carbon dioxide into the atmosphere, reducing climate change. Right now, the U.S. gets 7 percent of its energy from renewable sources; that number has to be a lot higher.

Renewable energy is sometimes a little more expensive than nonrenewable energy, because the technology that turns it into useful things like fuel for cars and electricity isn't that good yet. But lots of research is being done on renewable energy technologies, so they'll get cheaper, and in the long run, renewables are better for the planet.

Sustainable Lifestyles in a Changing Economy **49**

BIG STEPS
Living Smaller, Living Slower

So far, you've made small changes in your life like turning off lights, recycling, and eating less meat. If you feel strongly about limiting your impact on the planet, then you might be ready to make bigger changes in your life.

If you still ride in a car and live in an average house, you are unfortunately still having a negative impact on the planet as far as resource use goes. That doesn't mean you're a bad person, it just means that it takes a lot of effort to live in an environmentally friendly way. Not many people today have acheived that goal, so you're in good company.

Where you live also has a lot to do with how sustainable you are. People who live in places where food crops grow without too much help from food and water, for example,

are more sustainable just because of where they live, not because of how they live.

Ultimately, you have to put some more effort into making your life completely sustainable. Living smaller and living slower is a good motto to follow. People who live entirely sustainable lives buy much less stuff and instead repair things that are broken, or buy all used items. They also live slower, using public transportation or bikes to get places, and they don't mind spending time canning food and skipping the fast-food lines. It's not for everyone, but it's a worthy goal.

What Is Wealth?

There are two ways to think about wealth. The first thing that pops into a lot of people's heads is money. Wealth equals a lot of money and affluence; essentially it means you're rich. You can also think of wealth in terms of other resources besides money. Having a lot of free time makes you wealthy in terms of time, and having a lot of good friends makes you rich in friendship. Wealth is more like an abundance of something, though we normally associate it with an abundance of money.

Sustainable living addresses both ways of thinking about wealth. If you practice sustainable finances now, you'll grow your savings. If you're really good at managing your money, you could someday become modestly rich. Sustainable living also teaches you how to consider yourself wealthy in non-monetary terms. By focusing on your friends and family, your garden, and your impact on the Earth, you'll be richer in relationships, skills, knowledge, and hopefully, happiness.

Sustainable Lifestyles in a Changing Economy 53

YOU AND THE PLANET

Personally changing your life is important, but it will only make a small difference in the world. The average individual has a tiny impact on the environment, but if everyone made changes in their lives, then all those tiny impacts add up to one big change. If no one made the tiny changes you're making, then there would be no hope we could improve the environment and stop climate change.

Don't be discouraged if you can't actually see the change you're making in the world by living more sustainably. Just be confident that every person who reduces her footprint on Earth is contributing to a better world by working together. As more and more people practice sustainable living, you'll start to see changes like a reduction in climate change, flourishing animal and plant life, and better world health. Plus, you'll definitely notice the difference sustainable living will make on your finances.

Once you get the hang of sustainable living, you can live knowing that you have a little extra pocket money, that you've learned responsible money management, and that you're doing the right thing for the environment and the people around you.

Here's What You Need to Remember

- Living sustainably means making sure you and the rest of the world have enough resources to live comfortably in the future. That entails limiting your use of resources today.

- Sustainable living is good for the environment and your wallet. By trying to limit your resource use, you also save a lot of money because you buy fewer things and use the things you do buy more wisely.

- One of the most important steps toward sustainability is figuring out what you need and what you want. Once you determine that, you can focus on the things that you need in life.

- Beware of advertising and impulse buying, which makes you purchase things you don't really need or want. Make a goal of living sustainably, and stick to it.

- There are lots of things you can do to live more sustainably. Small steps include recycling, saving energy, buying secondhand goods, and changing your diet. Bigger steps include limiting your use of nonrenewable energy and living a slower, smaller life.

Words You Need to Know

byproducts: Materials left over from a chemical process (like oil refining) or the manufacture of a product from raw materials.

credit report: A report containing detailed information on a person's financial history, credit card accounts, loans, bankruptcies, and late payments that is used by potential lenders to determine if that person is a good risk to lend money or give credit to.

culture: The behaviors, customs, and beliefs of a particular group of people, such as American culture or Mexican culture.

disposable income: The extra money that is still available to spend after all of a person's necessities (food, rent, clothing, etc.) are paid for.

droughts: Long periods of little or no water supplies, usually caused by lack of rainfall.

extracting: The removal of a natural resource from its original location (as in drilling for oil or coal mining) for human use.

footprint: The total effect a person has on the Earth, determined by the amount of natural resources they use and the pollution and waste they produce.

infrastructures: The basic systems and services needed by a community, such as transportation, communication, water and power lines, schools, and hospitals.

negotiable: A decision or agreement that is flexible enough to be easily changed.

organic: Food products, such as fruits, vegetables, or meat, that are raised using natural methods that create a minimum of pollution and waste.

realistic: Goals and expectations that are not unlikely in a particular situation.

recession: A period of time when the economy is doing badly and people have less money to spend.

resources: Materials that are produced by the Earth, such as water, oil, natural gas, and plant and animal life, that human beings use for various purposes.

Further Reading

Earthworks Group. *50 Simple Things Kids Can Do to Recycle*. New York: Earthworks Press, 2004.

Harman, Hollis Page. *Money Sense for Kids*. Hauppauge, New York: Barron's Educational Services, Inc., 2004.

Schlosser, Eric. *Fast Food Nation*. New York: Harper Collins, 2002.

Schwartz, Ellen. *I'm a Vegetarian: Amazing Facts and Ideas for Healthy Vegetarians*. New York: Tundra Books, 2004.

Find Out More
On the Internet

Center for Sustainable Systems
css.snre.umich.edu/facts/factsheets.html

Global Issues: Consumption and Consumerism
www.globalissues.org/issue/235/consumption-and-consumerism

Natural Resources Defense Council: Green Living
www.nrdc.org/greenliving

Simple Projects To Reduce Your Energy Costs
greenteam.ky.gov/projects.htm

US Environmental Protection Agency
www.epa.gov/sustainability

The websites listed on this page were active at the time of publication. The publisher is not responsible for websites that have changed their address or discontinued operation since the date of publication. The publisher will review and update the websites upon each reprint.

Index

Picture Credits

About the Author and Consultant

Rae Simons is a well-established educational author, who has written on a variety of topics for young adults for the past twenty years. She has also worked with financial advisors to produce adult-level books on money management.

Brigitte Madrian is Professor of Public Policy and Corporate Management in the Aetna-Chair at Harvard University's Kennedy School of Government. She has also been on the faculty at the Wharton School and the University of Chicago. She is also a Research Associate at the National Bureau of Economic Research and coeditor of the *Journal of Human Resources*. She is the first-place recipient of the National Academy of Social Insurance Dissertation Prize and the TIAA-CREF Paul A. Samuelson Award for Scholarly Research on Lifelong Financial Security.